BLADE BY BLADE

T0286569

ALSO BY DANUSHA LAMÉRIS

Bonfire Opera

The Moons of August

BLADE BY BLADE

DANUSHA LAMÉRIS

COPPER CANYON PRESS
PORT TOWNSEND, WASHINGTON

Cover art: A blade of grass with a serrated edge (*Paspalum* sp), colored scanning electron micrograph (SEM). Photo credit: Dennis Kunkel Microscopy/Science Photo Library.

Copper Canyon Press is in residence at Fort Worden State Park in Port Townsend, Washington, under the auspices of Centrum. Centrum is a gathering place for artists and creative thinkers from around the world, students of all ages and backgrounds, and audiences seeking extraordinary cultural enrichment.

LIBRARY OF CONGRESS CATALOGING-IN-PUBLICATION DATA
Names: Laméris, Danusha, author.
Title: Blade by blade / Danusha Laméris.
Description: Port Townsend, Washington : Copper Canyon Press, 2024. |
    Summary: "A collection of poems by Danusha Laméris"— Provided by
    publisher.
Identifiers: LCCN 2024014867 (print) | LCCN 2024014868 (ebook) |
    ISBN 9781556597039 (paperback) | ISBN 9781619323087 (epub)
Subjects: LCGFT: Poetry.
Classification: LCC PS3612.A54685 B53 2024 (print) |
    LCC PS3612.A54685 (ebook) | DDC 811/.6—dc23/eng/20240404
LC record available at https://lccn.loc.gov/2024014867
LC ebook record available at https://lccn.loc.gov/2024014868

9 8 7 6 5 4 3 2 FIRST PRINTING

COPPER CANYON PRESS
Post Office Box 271
Port Townsend, Washington 98368
www.coppercanyonpress.org

for Armando & Pumpkin

What hasn't

been rent, divided, split? Broken
the days into nights, the night sky

into stars, the stars into patterns
I make up as I trace them

with a broken-off blade
of grass.

DORIANNE LAUX, "What's Broken," *Facts About the Moon*

CONTENTS

3

4

BLADE BY BLADE

Barefoot

I learned the world through the bottoms of my feet, bare
in the creeks of summer, stepping on pebbles, the squidge
of moss between my toes. On hot asphalt, the hop and skip
over cracks, feet already toughened by bramble, dirt, the prickly
ground of pine needles. Calloused and ready to roam the rough halls
of July, of August, of early September, through acres of blackberry
and bristled fountain grass, the spiny clumps of cocklebur
and foxtail. Through clusters of quartz, agate, feldspar.
Black ants crawled over my toes. Fish nibbled at them
in the skinny creek. It wasn't summer until I'd been bitten,
ankles pocked with the raised bumps left by mosquitoes,
flea bites from Toof Toof the cat, who liked to rove the field,
then settle back on the shag rug, where I'd sink my toes into the plush
pile before rambling down to the beach, the fine-ground sand,
cutting myself on loose shards of glass left by broken beer bottles,
sharp-edged shells that dug into the fatted flesh of my sole
as I skimmed for washed-up bits of abalone, oyster, clam,
sidestepping the glutinous bodies of jellyfish, past crusted bulbs
of kelp, their long, tubed stems buzzing with flies. Sometimes,
the body of a dead seal, the peppered fin curling into itself in the heat.
Back on the grassy slope, I'd marvel at how I could feel
a gopher stir underground from yards away, that slight
rumble in the earth. This was foot-knowledge, heel-knowledge,
knowledge of sole and arch, that domed curve, vaulted nave,
everything that entered there, sanctified, holy.

Fire Season

Meanwhile the motorcycles
churr down Pacific Avenue,
revved and ready to head north
up Highway 1, past the rough
surf and golden cliffs, past
small towns held together
by roadside restaurants serving up
burgers and artichoke bisque,
the pelicans hanging low
on the late-day wind
above the corrugated line
of the horizon. It's the season
of fire, but all I can see is water,
water running out as far
as the stitched hem of sky.
An epoch of water
lying low under the white-
capped waves.
I have wanted to live
in this paradise forever,
to dwell here on this
cracked continental edge
inhaling the fragrance
of salt and seaweed,
stepping on the loose
gravel leading down
to the shore, waters
in which I was baptized by
a wild froth of surf
that filled my eyes, my ears,
my mouth as I tumbled

shoreward. If I belong anywhere,
it's here on this scorched
rib of field leading to the sand.
Walcott once said
the frame of human happiness
is time. Then frame me here,
caught in the early days
of autumn, in this teetering era,
a hint of smoke in the air.

Construction

I remember downtown after the earthquake—
piles of rubble, metal gates set up to corral us in the
middle of the road so we wouldn't step on all that
broken concrete, on pediments fallen from doorways,
makeshift memorials to people who died under the debris.
Sometimes you'd pass a building's facade held up
with beams, the rest of the structure gone. An empty
lot visible through the blown-out windows.
I know that place, that saving what I can. OK,
I lost my house but I'm alive. Or OK, my brother died,
but I'm living twice—no, three times—for me, for him,
and for my son. I saved the front of the building,
its delicate arches and raised friezes. I didn't hate it.
You could still buy socks or get coffee
in these giant tents that popped up in the ruins.
That's aftermath for you. The way we keep on drinking
out of little paper cups, walking through disaster
in our brand-new shoes for everyone who can't.

Blue Note

My brother named all his houseplants after jazz musicians,
so when he left town he'd say, Can you water Miles?
Coltrane is getting too cold by the window. Give Billie
a little extra drizzle, but let her dry out. Was there
a Nina? I can't remember. But I know Mingus had
broad, glossy leaves and Cassandra, a pink tint
to her foliage, was frail due to less-than-tropical conditions.
I'm trying to say it was music and plants and sprouted greens
and my brother in the kitchen, chef-ing up roasted beets
and everyone hanging out, old-style Oakland, which was
wood floors and hummus and take-out Ethiopian. I thought
we'd live like kings. A dynasty, from one potluck to the next.
It felt that way. The red-carpet days of our twenties.
I took care of those plants as best I could, put them
in my own living room, gave them liquid fertilizer and,
I hoped, the right slant of light. I thought we'd gotten out
beyond the worst of it—the story we were born to. Though
we both had a feeling he'd die young. But the years kept ticking,
and the friends kept coming, and his children arrived,
curled and new in their cribs. It was hard to notice things
beginning to turn, to see the signs. The mind's erasure.
He started checking the locks, closing curtains, talking in low tones.
Sometimes the leaves start to yellow and you don't even notice.
There's a sound absence makes, even before it arrives,
a static in the ether, high and blue and held.

Nocturne

The past is a country of darkness, its long nights
and arctic sun slung low over the horizon.
The young woman you were, rising early, washing up
the dishes left in the sink, attending to the kettle's
high-pitched wail. You can't go back there,
even as a passenger, can't ride the night rails
to find yourself locked in that long-ago loop—
the drive to the hospital and back, the child still caught
midseizure, the doctor with the telepathic touch,
leaning over him with a needle to pierce his invisible veins.
Time, honeyed and slow, the nurse setting out
the warm towels, the man in the next cubicle
yelling, "You can't make me!" in his torn voice,
his feral beard pointing north. Look at the nurse,
her blue scrubs, her small pearl earrings.
The doctor's pressed shirt and placid brow. As if
we'd all arrived dressed for the occasion
of death. Look at my son's black hair. See how
we hover there at the edge of it, the stars
barely visible through the window, small
specks ticking the dark, fixed in place.

Daughter

I always wanted a daughter, which is
to say, I wanted a better self,

flicked from my marrow—made
flesh. I wanted this bone-of-my-bones

to move in the world, exceptional
and unharmed. Not this world. But a world

almost exactly unlike it. Same
paved streets and street cafés, same slow

unfurl of spring. Only, in that world,
the green of field and orchard is still wanton

with winged things, their bellies powdered
with the flowers' gold dust.

Daughter, I say, and I mean a list
of what-ifs, a cacophony of sorrows.

I imagine her tall, lithe as willows.
When I say Daughter,

I mean a match, ready to strike herself
against the world that isn't

this one. I mean luck. I mean a river
empty of drowning. I mean an arrow

aimed at an unnamed star. Someone
once said a daughter is a needle in the heart.

I would take that needle, sew her a dress
of yarrow and blood.

In the world not this one,
I have a daughter. She is a long braid,

a memory of fire. She goes before me,
shining darkly, into a city—

of gold, of salt—that I will never see.

Okra

My mother used to wash them in our old,
nicked colander, then drop them
in a pan of bubbling cornmeal.

I recall the quick work of her hands,
the way she held the knife
beneath her thumb, took the sticky pods
and sliced them in the air.

Butter. Pepper. Salt. And memory.
Whose mother's mother's mother's
gift was this, and in what forgotten country?

To her, it was island food, *cou cou,*
the name for okra made this way
and, if you were lucky,

served with a sliver of flying fish.
Taste of home to her. To me, flavor
of somewhere I had only been.

Impossible to count backward, trace.
Our line broken by ships.

Instead, the memory of hand and blade.
The evidence that blood requires.

If you cannot give me the past,
give me, at least, the taste.

Slither

I'd bring them home in jars, in my bare hands,
or sometimes wound around my arms: garter snakes
with their sleek yellow stripes, dull brown lizards,
their spiny toes and jagged sides. Once, a baby ring-necked snake,
no bigger than my pinkie, wearing its thin choker of coral.

In Barbados, at my grandparents', it was novelty I loved—
to reach into the dark water of the pond until I felt
the telltale bumps on the back of a cane toad.
I'd tuck my hands beneath, cup its weight in my palms.

But mostly, it was the backyard bounty of Northern California:
sagebrush lizards, pond turtles, the blue-tailed western skink.

Sometimes I grabbed one, was left only with
the tail. Sometimes one bit me and I wore a crescent
of teeth marks on the arc of my hand, between pointer and thumb.

But just last summer, when I found a frog under my bed
and reached for it, I shrieked when it leapt in midair
and its wet and bulbous body met my grasp.

It was then I knew I'd become a stranger to the world.
Gone, the self that grew from mud, ate bugs, dug holes
along the wet shore just to feel the legs of sand crabs graze her palms.

The girl who'd eat snails straight from the garden,
pluck them from the beds of tulips, put them in her mouth,
chew the wet flesh, the crunchy shell.

Snail Girl. Slug Girl. Snake Girl. I wish
I could slip back into her small body, feel my knees
in the damp grass. Go back into the green, green world.

Or even into the one before. When I was small as the curve
of a spoon, hidden in the body of my mother, slick and gilled—
ready to begin again. To enter the realm I'd know by its
soft loam, dark water, rough dirt. To start over,
leaf by leaf, blade by beckoning blade.

2

They Say the Heart Wants

what it wants, but no one tells you what it gets.
So here's a list, mine: tall grasses blowing in the wind,

swirled glass cups, peacock blue, bought in Lebanon.
Fog off the California cliffs, dark boulders on the shore.

Billie Holiday's *I'll be seeing you in all the old
familiar places* cycling through my auditory cortex.

Dogs pulling at the leash. Small white plates
of wild greens and beets. The time a man kissed

my hand when we met, then pressed my palm
to his cheek. Sei Shōnagon's eleventh-century list

of "Things That Give One a Clean Feeling": an earthen cup,
a new metal bowl, a rush mat, the play of light on water

as one pours it into a vessel, a new wooden chest.
To which I add a drawer of beeswax candles,

steam rising from a pot of tea. So much stored
in the heart's farthest chambers. And though

he's been dead for decades now, I still feel the kiss.
My whole arm shivers with its half-life.

The Kissing Disease

Isn't that what they called it? The fever
you could catch from pressing your lips
to the lips of another in the dark corner
of the gym after the game, or later,
lying down in the rough bramble
of the field. And then a long malaise—
a month in bed, swollen glands
of the neck. You had to sip hot fluids,
eat crackers laced with salt, lie down
until it passed. What a way to meet
the god of want, slack deity who slips
into the back of your throat, microscopic
germ. The way we learn desire
is a contagion cast from one body
to the next. Something you contract
by getting close enough to inhale
the whiff of musk rising from her
like a lick of flame. Or from feeling
his shirt shake beneath your palm—
the dizzy of his heart. Bitter particle,
trick spore. Microbe hidden
in the volcano of the mouth.
Malady of the young, virus
of the tonsil, the tongue. What
can we say of how it enters the blood,
scorches a path through the veins,
sickens us with hunger, shapes
the course of what's to come.

The Cows of Love Creek

are eating corncobs from our hands,
their soft mouths grazing our fingertips,

tongues torqued sideways. We offer apples,
lower them through the wire-strung fence,

and they take them, eyes widening at the rush
of sweetness. And, for a moment, we're in love,

not only with each other, but with their wet
and gentle nostrils, their twitchy ears and busy jaws,

the way they munch the goodness of summer,
bellies fattened by clover, by dried hay and dandelion,

the scrub that flattens, easily, beneath their hooves.
If I could, I'd name them Goldenrod, Cocklebur, Tansy—

after the sparse blooms that decorate the field.
They are only a year old, not far past suckling.

Yet look how they take the world in. A hunger
to feast on the light falling along the meadow.

On the slender pines circling the field. An earlobe,
folded, furred. My beloved stands in the trees' long shadows.

We watch the swoosh of their tails, admire the chestnut
of this one, the dapple of another, feed them cob

and ripe fruit, touch the tufts of fur that sprout
from their crowns. I do not want to say love

is like devouring. But devouring is like love.
Just last winter we accepted the gift

of beef from this very ranch, sliced
into the tender red meat, laced with salt.

I bend to pick another windfall apple, offer it
to the nearest wet tongue grazing my palm.

We cannot love the earth
without getting blood on our hands.

Alphabet of the Apocalypse

Where does an end begin? Why not with *A*—
Atlantis sinking back into the sea with its
aquatic spires and crystal architecture.

B for herds of bison whittled down
to almost nothing, drinking from
the drying lake.

I don't know when the body's cells
decide to give up the ghost. How they
start to catapult toward decay.

Death knell of the form, its
sweet and terrible diminishment.
First decrease, then end.

Snowy egrets, standing in a glade.
Eagles, elephants, elk. The late pink light
through groves of eucalyptus.

Great green planet, formerly known
as Earth—Will you end in fire?
What will they call you when we're gone?

Who will be left to sit beneath
the moon's nightly glow? Who will
recall the glacier's tall blue countenance?

Here on Earth as it is in Heaven. But
isn't heaven a white expanse of
nothing capped with nothing?

So much for the ibex, its long-pronged horns.
So much for Italy, iguanas, the iris, the color
indigo, steeped in vats in rural India.

So much for June, month of brides
clasping cut flowers—orange blossoms, jasmine,
coral-colored roses—in their careful hands.

I've never been to Kansas or seen a kangaroo,
though once a katydid hid in my curtain,
and sang, all night, its little virgin song.

O Lamb, O Lion, it matters little now
whether you lie together,
on the bare and ruined soil.

Mother, mountain, mammary.
No more, these founts
for mammals and mystics.

It was never enough: nectar from the orchard,
nightingales singing from the highest boughs.
Narwhals decorating the northern seas.

Once, I took a child to the ocean
for the first time. I can't forget the sound
she made, that gasp—her mouth an *O*.

Wouldn't it be better if we'd all stayed
pagan, stunned each night at the moon,
the trembling stars.

If we quivered, still, at the unlikely
grass, the song in the river, the shimmer
on the face of cut stone.

What if we remembered the shy soul
in everything—the world shot through
with whistle and hum.

If we sought, above all, the silence
between blades of green, the pause
inside the cricket's choir.

To touch the tender core of Things,
and tell of it. Pure pleasure.
What more could we want?

To undress the world, get close
to its shiver, rock and spore, river
and bark, the dandelion's naked stem.

Our vagabond planet, traveling
the galaxy's milky arm,
pulled by forces we can't see—

with *us:* wanderers, wanters,
those who crave. Always restless
for the next and next.
Following the x-axis
of some trajectory we can't know.
To be or not?

Which brings me here to the window,
looking out at the acacia, blooming acid yellow
in the field beside my house.

This moment, the zillionth, in a long parade.
A something arising from nothing.
Existing. And sinking back, again.

There

When we arrive—if we arrive—
it's always the ordinary: dead leaves
on the drive, salamanders nesting
under the firewood stacked by the barn,
the barn's chipped paint, light falling
slant over the rabbited field. Once,
I thought there was a *there,*
but there wasn't. Only *this.*
Let this, then, be there's eulogy.
Bury it in the hard earth of the once-was
orchard, drop it down the well,
send it down the creek on a raft
of kindling and flame. What's left: air
filling and unfilling the plush cavity
of your chest, a little wind in the alders,
the neighbor hauling two-by-fours to the side
of the house, hammering them together,
that echo of metal against wood.

Everything Is Old

Everything is old. The sea with its ancient
lament, birds left over from dinosaurs, their
pterodactyl bones. Rocks, their long, molten histories
and imprints of ancient fish. The trees ringed
with years of lean, years of plenty. Who needs to name
the elephants with their wizened eyes and swinging gait,
the sadness that glazes their leathery hides.
The sun is older than we want to think, already
past midlife, its years of fusion finite. Old
the song that lifts between two bodies in the dark.
Old the rain, the snow, the fox, hiding in its den. Old
the long hours awake in the middle of the night.
Old the night, and old the moon. Old the sound of awe
we make watching it rise, full, over the trees. The vowels
we cry are old, once pictographs on papyrus.
The language is old, dying even as we write it down.
Who will decipher our sorrow, who will know
our joy. Though these, too, are old, and unlikely
to alter. Why not take an old, chipped cup, fill it
with water, or, for that matter, the fermented
leaves of something aged, a little bruised, ripened
in a cave. Why not take a sip, and sit awhile
in silence, its weighted grace the oldest thing of all.

Leg

We're walking around the field by my house, Dion and I—
her dog pulling at the leash, collecting, no doubt, an array
of ticks in her bristly white fur—when we come upon
the half-eaten leg of a deer, gnawed clean along the thigh bone,
the calf still covered in its thin scrim of flesh and tawny fur.
The dark hoof, a fatted arrow pointing uphill toward where,
we imagine, the rest of the deer might lie—a doe, I'm thinking—
deep in a grove of eucalyptus, carried off in the jaws
of a mountain lion. Dion pokes at the bone,
says, Don't you want to keep it! Look at that hoof!

The dog rolls around in the nearby grass, basking
in the afterdeath, wanting to carry a whiff of it
like a fine cologne. We keep circling the field,
coming upon fresh remains: the russet feathers of a hen,
fanned out, the plasticky stems still wadded together.
Past coyote scat. Then back to the leg. I turn to Dion, say,
I think it's yours. Take it.

She's had some parts replaced. At least one hip. I'm hobbling
a little on my bad ankle. Even on a good day, we're both fair game.
I look down the hill at the rusted tractor, fruit fallen
from the apple trees, haloed by a buzz of wasps.

We walk farther up the slope, over thistles and clumps
of dandelion, lean down to the stippled earth
and revel in its decadent decay.

It's hot. The dog digs at a gopher hole. A hundred
miles away my sister-in-law is growing a small bouquet
of errant cells in her left lung. Others on her spine, her ribs.
No one else has her exact rasp of voice, her hands,

their stacked gold rings, her freezer full of turkey broth,
her wonky, bunioned big toe. Her long black hair.

Her life, the one she kept on living after
my brother died. Catching babies, cutting the rubbery cord,
wiping the bloody vernix from their brows.

I think of how I've come to call her sister, dropping
the suffix. We've known each other since
she was three and I was six. And I don't know
what a sister is if not an other, a fragile mirror, space
of tenderness. Female, and mortal, and afraid.

I watch as Dion takes a stick and digs around
in the same hole as the dog, who is now sniffing the loose dirt.
Sisters, I think, of the two of them, the woman and the dog,
happily engaged in their unburying.

And somehow, walking in silence, back the way we came,
sisters, I name the two of us, me and Dion,
rounding the path down the hill, back home.

And when I eye, again, the doe's skinned leg
lying in the loam, I think, for a moment, sister,
of the scrap that's left.

But it's only later, lying awake in the dark,
that I picture the tawny shadow
skimming the hillside, hidden by a clump of trees.
Sister, I think, of the lion that ate her.

Lava

Once, two women hiked a volcano,
stood on the lip and watched the fire
move in the crater's mouth.

Neither spoke. Not even when the ground
began to shake and they felt the rumble
through their soles and up their legs.

They just stood there, eyes fixed.
Later, both admitted the truth: each fought
an urge to leap.

What is it we could give our lives for?
A mountain, a fire, a view from the cliff.

Every year, on the coast where I live,
tourists die, amazed
by the Monterey Bay, swept from the shelf
of rock overlooking the waves.

And farther north, some people get
so close to grizzly bears, they end up
taking their stories with them
into the darkness of the animal itself,

surrendering to its life of fur and forage,
to lumber through the woods at night,
becoming, at last, a gorgeous, insatiable beast.

Prayer to Be Undone

Great One, Maker, Weaver of Things, I want to undress the tree
to find you hidden there in the layers of sapwood, as you were hidden
in a mango I ate today, its sweet and buttery flesh. A fly entered the house
through the front door. Was that you? At sunset a coyote limped
across the field, looking back over its shoulder. I am trying to discern you.
I am trying to keep the door of my soul open so you can enter.
Sometimes I wake up late at night, the sheets cool against my skin,
and ask, Why have I been torn from the tapestry of petal, scrub, and bark?
But the sky is silent. The universe is one rhymed thing, but I keep
wanting to rhyme with *I, I*—to capitalize myself, stand apart from the whole.
I know I am a cloth and someday you will pull my thread,
unravel me—please unravel me—with your deft, invisible hands.

Appointment

I'm leaned back on the table, the nurse strapping
a cuff around my bicep, when she smiles, says,
So, your son must be thirteen by now. No, I say,
he's dead, which is harsher than I mean to say it.
Oh! she says, your chart. Yes, I say. His birth,
the year. And now she feels bad. I'm sorry, she says,
I'm so sorry. It's OK, I tell her, but the reading is too high,
the pressure. We'll try and do it again, she says.
Again. Again. The times I step back into the story,
and in this story my son is still living inside
me, he's aquatic. I am the fishbowl and he is
the fish. I imagine his bones, his lungs, the small
perfect heart. His hands, his feet. A body
growing inside another body. So precise.
And then he's on the outside and it doesn't work:
The air. Gravity. I want to apologize. He can't breathe
right, he keeps convulsing, the electric
surge ticking his head to the left, the left, his
lip curled in disgust, but no, he looks more afraid—
some terror coming toward him. Not blue, not blue,
I tell myself the times it happens and he isn't.
The doctor says, The bad kind of blue is cobalt, Smurf blue.
Dusky is not the worst kind. But how does she know
on a baby this shade of brown? I'm sorry,
I'm so sorry, I tell him in the hospital again,
but he can't hear me because of the sedative
and the new doctor is asking me, Can a student insert
a long needle into his spinal column.
I look out the window and see plants, a garden.
Our nurse comes in, says, There's another garden
on the roof. You can go look. Just don't jump off.

The story is a circle that repeats, a round,
the voices overlapping. He's in my arms again,
my baby, my baby, I am singing to him.
I kiss his cheek, his hair. And now he's not thirteen.
He's not anything. The nurse has left and I'm alone.
On the ceiling is a lake, a field of flowers.
Let's try this again, I say to no one.
I'm still here. I'm lying on the table, looking up.

Nothing Wants to Suffer

after Linda Hogan

Nothing wants to suffer. Not the wind
as it scrapes itself against the cliff. Not the cliff

being eaten, slowly, by the sea. The earth does not want
to suffer the rough tread of those who do not notice it.

The trees do not want to suffer the axe, nor see
their sisters felled by root rot, mildew, rust.

The coyote in its den. The puma stalking its prey.
These, too, want ease and a tender animal in the mouth

to take their hunger. An offering, one hopes,
made quickly, and without much suffering.

The chair mourns an angry sitter. The lamp, a scalded moth.
A table, the weight of years of argument.

We know this, though we forget.

Not the shark nor the tiger, fanged as they are.
Nor the worm, content in its windowless world

of soil and stone. Not the stone, resting in its riverbed.
The riverbed, gazing up at the stars.

Least of all, the stars, ensconced in their canopy,
looking down at all of us—their offspring—

scattered so far beyond reach.

3

Praying Mantis

At first, I saw it in my garden, clinging
to the fence behind a rosebush. Later,
it appeared beside me in the grass.
This went on—for weeks. A month.
I can't be sure. I'd never seen one up close.
Bright green, boggle eyed, the odd,
nearly automated movement. It seemed
almost prescient. Diviner. Alien. Priest.
What would we know if our eyes could rotate
behind as well as ahead. The roses
were in bloom. Everything appeared as it
should be: Grass trimmed, floors swept,
a bowl of fruit on the kitchen table.
My husband humming to himself
as he walked from room to room.
Everyone I loved was alive. Sometimes,
I felt those eyes press into the back
of my neck, follow me as I
weeded the yard. Then one day
I woke up and it was on the ceiling,
hind legs hooked into the canopy
above the bed. Poised, perfectly still.
Forelimbs held in that chronic gesture
of supplication. It looked down at me,
head cocked, a cool expression—
clean and pitiless.

How Often One Death

How often one death carries another. Like when
my painting teacher, Eduardo, died and the cat

he'd had for years succumbed the same month
to the same rare ailment. Or how when they buried

my friend's grandfather in Japan, the pondful of koi
he'd tended all his life sickened, turned belly up.

Who or what is in our keeping? A house, unoccupied,
quickly sinks into itself, turns earthward.

Long-married couples are known to give up
the ghost within hours of each other.

Think of the hum that holds the walls together,
the roof high, keeps the rot at bay a little longer.

As surely as we, too, are pinned here by others,
whose presence urges our cells to replicate, our lives

more bound than we imagine. Even the woman I can't see,
who lives in a studio on the other side of the wall.

She washes a dish and the water runs through the pipes
between us, like blood through the arteries of a single heart.

For the Record

It's been thirteen years since my brother died,
and I'm still afraid of his shirts, his leather jacket,
his cologne, the letter he sent that arrived, after.
His scrawled script with oversized, looped *g*'s. I don't
want to look at the death certificate I keep
in a blue folder, its official seal, and black type.

I don't want to talk about his body in the back seat—
or was it the front seat? I don't know where
it happened, only that he aimed for his heart
and not his face. I don't know what street it was, or
what city or if I ever want to know
whose house he parked in front of, or why that house.
Someone he hoped would find him.
The car was a black BMW, the seats leather. And, after,
the husband of a friend cleaned up the blood.

I haven't written his obituary, even though I could,
even though I think it would be the right thing to do, to
leave a record, even though my mother wanted me to,
but now she's dead and I haven't written hers either.

The dead are helpless. They can't make you do things
you don't want to do. I don't want to write an obituary
for a dead person who wanted me to write an obituary
for another dead person. So even if it makes me a bad person,
a failed one, I don't want to make myself do it, to try and fit
their lives into narrow columns of born here, schooled there,
the husband, the wife, the town, et cetera. I don't want to talk
about who remembers them, who survives them, who survives.

Boy

Somewhere a boy is trying to sleep on the floor
of a room crowded with children he doesn't know.
Somewhere a man and woman weep for him. When I close
my eyes, I can almost reach out to touch that child's hair.
Or, at least, that's what I tell myself. That at this hour of night,
there's a way to join one solitude to another. And because
I was once a child taken from my mother—not by strangers,
but by a father who thought my brother and I were his
to take across state lines and keep in a condo littered with dog scat,
stale dishes, and the low ache of fear—I want to think there could
have been someone I did not know who imagined me, who
wished me solace. Or, better yet, who would lift me
from those dingy rooms where he'd leave us while he went
to the store for beer, to work, to see a woman.
I'll never know. Once, my brother toddled out onto the deck
and peed on the path below. It's the face of the guard
I remember, his grimace. *You can't do that,* he said, though
he never asked why we were alone. Two small children,
one no more than three. Looking back, what I don't
want to see—this was the South—is how color is a character
in this story. Two brown-skinned kids, unkempt. Our hair
unbrushed. The baby naked and peeing through the wrought-iron
railing. Did we register to him as human? Animal?
Sometimes for dinner my brother ate a tortilla filled
with sugar. Some days, we sat outside in the courtyard
and ate watermelon. You see where I am going.
Tonight, as every night, the boy's stomach aches.
He is afraid. He does not know if he will have to live
here forever. If he's been forgotten. If he'll ever see his mother.
I do not want to think of how he holds the sheet,
the regulation blanket, to his chest. Of what is breaking

inside him. What is torn does not mend the same.
When my brother unwound and we laid him in his early grave,
we said it was hereditary. Many things are inherited.
Whole histories, for example—and the long paths walked in the heat,
in the dead of night—away from them. This is what we will say
when the boy asks, should he live to ask: *This is your inheritance.*
O God of the Dark Night, Angel of Emptiness, whatever
has kept me here, broken as I am, whatever you are,
please be more than our own ruin. Run some river of salvation
through that boy's blood, his bones. And another through us all.

Clydesdales

Walking downtown in December,
I think I hear tap dancers,
picture them trussed up in fishnets
and frill, jazzing the sidewalk
with their slick shoes. But
when I look and see
instead a pair of horses
pulling a white carriage
down the avenue,
their great tufted hooves
clipping the dark,
rain-soaked street, I stop
to admire them as they pass:
blond manes and thick flanks,
accompanied by the warm,
earthen odor of manure—
a mix of stimuli that
sends my senses keening
for a world I never even knew—
rustling petticoats, damp hay,
the squeak of iron. As if
such things were locked
in our genes, some code
for carriage, horse,
that clappered
gait. Or as if there were
a horse-shaped pit
in the soul, a gap
we live with
like so many
other things we

don't even know
we miss: the night sky
before we dimmed the stars,
sitting under them,
around a fire. And
the something else
we cannot name—
oh—but we once
cried for it, wordless,
inconsolable,
in our mother's arms.

The Sound

I'm not sure if I want to tell you this, but
it's only a story, and like all stories, it's held
in time. It begins with death. My son's
off life support. The doctors wheeling him
into the OR to harvest his still-living organs.

He was not conscious. He had, I told myself,
already vacated the frame, something
he'd been close to doing since he was born.

I sat at home alone on the couch while the surgeons,
no doubt with great care, severed him from his heart,
his kidneys, his liver. I don't want to know what else.
I could not think about it, and so, instead,
I closed my eyes, imagined him a wisp, a breath
of air moving upward, out of the confines
of the body.

And then, I heard it, a humming that seemed
to be everywhere at once, but not everywhere.
For a moment, I couldn't say if the sound was coming
from inside, as a sound might, in a dream, seem to arise
from inside the dreamer. But then it was clear
that it was outside and circling the house—a song
of arrows—and all at once, I saw them, the one body
they made, a kinetic cloud at the window,
those wound-givers, honey-makers,

and something like fear rose in me. Would they enter
the house? I must have risen, crossed the room
to close the window, though I don't remember.
They moved as one, the whole of them,

a clustered orchestra. First, dense and singular,
then dispersed. Agile entity, both bound
and unbound. I watched them

hover like that until I could no longer
say what they were, if they were one or many,
or what—what, anymore—was a body.

4

Horse Heart

I keep going back in my mind,
down the path lined with ice plant
and coltsfoot still in bloom. Down
to the wet shore.

Me and S.—the months before
we knew he was dying. How
we walked the foggy beach and when
he looked away, in one quick
movement, I took off my dress,

so when he turned and saw me,
I was naked against the shore,
holding the dress above my head
like a flag.

And then, when we *did* know,
the two of us on that same stretch
of sand, pressed against
the crumbling edge of the continent.

Nothing left to salvage except
maybe the curve of his shoulder
under my palm. The ring of rust
around the green disk of his iris.

A few chestnut horses haunt
the hillside, tails twitching
in the morning haze, hooves
chafing the sad, abundant earth.

Wind

I hate how it howls
around the corners
of our house
tosses
branches against the dark
windows, bony fingers
scraping the glass. Or how
it rattles traffic lights,
twists street signs,
swings electric wires. Once,
on our way
to the airport when I was a girl,
a sudden gust
took our car,
slammed it
against the concrete divide.
I hate its mouthless,
lungless breath, its faceless
cry.
All want, want, want.
The way it wants
to subtract us
from ourselves—
isn't that what it's trying to do?
That tug and shove
as I drive the coast, threading
the rocky corridor
between cliff and sea. At night,
that hoarse whisper
when I'm trying to sleep.

It blows branches off the trees,
tears trees up by the roots.
The way a great love
will take you,
shake you loose,
strip you clean
with its large,
indifferent thirst.

To Break

You know. You were there. It was dark
and quiet. The coyotes howling up the hill.
You took my face in your hands,
held it like a cup, a chalice, something
from which you could drink. I've wanted that.
To be a well one might drink from, a font
to quench the thirst. And while the deer crept
into the front garden, buried their faces
in November's last blossoms, a light rain
began to fall upon the field. And because
it was dark, and because no one will speak of it—
what passed between us—I will press it here
to the page, a dried flower, a wild bloom,
where it will remain, caught, still fragrant.
How there was something your body
said to mine in its halting speech of torso
and bicep, its vocabulary of fire. And mine
tried to answer in its own fumbling dialect—
fingertip, collarbone, rib. I wanted to break
something inside you. Enter some fissure
in your soul, that dark room with its dirt floors
and melancholic choirs. To fall into that
underground cavern of you, forget, awhile,
the burnt taste of my own grief, the cracked
vessel of my heart. I thought I could free
whatever animal lurks there, paces
in the cave of your chest, tearing up
the dust. And you were descending
the ladder of my body, and the coyotes
were getting louder, and I could feel us
moving close to that abyss. But it was late,

and getting later, and we didn't need to peel off
another layer of old wants, to wake up
penitent, reeling. And so we let it go, rose
from our makeshift bed, blew out the flame.
And I know I should forget what happened,
but let me tell you, friend, though years
have passed, there are nights, like this one,
when I hear the deer's mouths
closing on the flowers, and I see you
leaning over me, again, and it's winter,
the candle lit, the rain just starting to fall.

The Bermuda Triangle

It loomed large over my childhood, hungry mouth
in the middle of the Atlantic, a vast expanse that ate boats—
dinghies, cargo ships—sucked them down below the waves.
Or maybe took them up, like the planes that vanished
in midair, nothing left, not even contrails icing the upper
atmosphere. Not even a slip of a pilot's lapel or piece
of fuselage fallen from the clouds.

I'd lie on the couch and watch its red outline hover
over the undulating map, learn the names of vessels
that went down without a trace: *Star Tiger,* a plane
bound for Bermuda, the USS *Cyclops,* its load of metal ore,
over three hundred people never found. Once, they said a passenger
flight turned a somersault in midair, nose over tail, then
righted itself and moved on. No way to know who or what

was behind it. Though now I know something of the pull
that can prove too great. Desire's lure. How murky
the waters of the heart, its rough, uncharted seas
and taut geometry. Who among us hasn't drifted into
that treacherous terrain, engines whirring, compass gone
suddenly amok, only clouds above us, only clouds below.

Ordinary Fires

Outside, the neighbors are running their tractors
across the still-green fields, while the kids next door
jump on a giant trampoline and shriek as they bounce up
into the afternoon air. Which, from downwind,
smells like freshly shorn grass, with notes of trash fire
and lilac. Could be worse.

A cup of tea, a book. The mind free to follow
its endless alleyways. Which mine does, now—thinking of how,
across town, you're probably taking a shower, or reading
quietly, alone, in your backyard studio. Close enough,
but a distance I can't cross.

Maybe you're sitting in your favorite chair, stroking your beard
in the fading afternoon light. Putting on your reading glasses
as you turn the pages, before you join your wife for dinner.
I imagine you're happy.

As I, too, am happy. Loved by a man who lowers himself
to kiss my neck, his hair grazing my cheek.
Such goodness, I know, is rare. Still, I remember
the way you would look at me by candlelight, take my face
in your hands, as if you could peer into my soul's dingy chambers,
sweep them clean. Or how, before bed, you'd watch me
massage fragrant oil onto my limbs, as if to memorize the gesture—
a key ritual in some not-yet-named religion.

The Stoics said it's good to acclimate ourselves
to the ordinary, lest we suffer the absence of the sublime.
Don't drink the best wine, they warned. Beware the finest cloth.
And I can see their point, since almost everything
isn't Machu Picchu, the Grand Canyon, or Paris. Not even Paris.

If you lived there, you'd still have to call a plumber
when the sink got clogged, or be the plumber who fixes it.

Even if you were here, I tell myself, in that other,
impossible life, mostly, it would be like this: not ecstasy,
but light falling against the rotting planks of the barn,
the foxtail growing weedy and tall out by the shed. Maybe
we'd bicker about whose turn it was to hang the laundry
on the sagging line or prune the blackberry ravaging
the back fence.

It's dusk. There's a hush falling across the field, and a quiet
enters me with such carefulness, I can feel it fill my lungs,
and then my whole being. If I could, I'd tell you this:
whatever happened between us in those darkened rooms,
in the rain-strewn field, it's still here.

There's the way fire softens coal, makes it porous.
Sometimes, it's almost exquisite now—wind
churning the leaves of the cottonwood, rustling
the shorn edges of the grass, brushing against my arm,
my neck, my own bare face.

Glass

It's the small things that haunt: Oranges,
because my mother used to peel them for me,
slip the rough sections in my mouth. Luckies,
because of the wayward boy who lit my first,
leaning against the railing of the pier. "O sole mio"
wafts up from the downstairs apartment.
Now it means *all* those summers.
Can't they just turn it off? I walk through
Queen Anne's lace in late September,
down to the cove where I used to meet
a man who was dying, that flower now
in my own vocabulary of loss. What doesn't
in time enter grief's lexicon? When I think of
our house after the fire, all I see are pools
of pink glass—once our ice-cream bowls—
melted on the ruins.

Haute Potato

after a cookbook by Jacqueline Pham

The cover promises puréed potatoes,
seasoned with bay leaves and ginger, blessed
with wine-steamed mussels, squid and tamarind,
garlic and goat cheese. Purple potatoes
cooked in duck fat, potato-filled phyllo cigars,
stuffed with ricotta and lemon.

You could almost forget the common potato,
dressed in its plain brown wrapper, its jacket
of burlap and silt. A last link, for many,
between life and death: Peruvian farmers
digging the steep sides of hills. The Irish
wintering on their blighted bounty.

Once, I read of a man—a child of war—
how on the brink of famine, his family
was given a bag of potatoes, which they ate,
boiled and baked, without butter or salt.

The way those small stores, filling a sack
leaned against the kitchen wall, spelled *survive*
in plain, root language, dirt from the field
still clinging to their skins.

Hair of the Dead

The Victorians were known to wear it in brooches,
pinned to the lapels of their dark wool coats.
Or in gold lockets, dangling between their breasts.

I keep it in boxes, in plastic bags, in white envelopes.
My brother's perfect coil. My son's black strands, silky
as when they first came in, that full head of hair, a surprise

on a baby. How common, once, the early death,
a backyard cemetery lined with ornate stones. A child
gone to scarlet fever, a wife to childbirth, Spanish flu.

Longfellow's wife caught fire, it's said, sealing
her children's hair in envelopes, the match she used
to melt the wax, fallen in the folds of her dress.

When I was a girl I rode horses without saddles
through the dry hills, clutched them by their manes—
those fine tethers—to hold on.

The Bugs of Childhood

Don't you remember them? Furred
caterpillar legs moving along your arm,
each follicle prickling beneath their touch.
A ladybug crumpling its underwings as it
tucked them back beneath its glossy shell.
Rows and rows of ants, hefting their
white eggs. The fly's head, antennae bent
under the careful work of forelegs
as it bathed its large composite eye.

One, no bigger than a speck, left tufts
of foam, another, a pool of green
in your palm. Some rolled themselves
into a pill-shaped ball at the slightest touch,
while others, no matter how you tried, refused.
What was it about the workings of their small
bodies, the click of the mandibles
or the steady pulse of the thorax, so nipped
at the center it seemed tied with string,
almost electric, the way they zipped
through the grass, sunlight caught
in iridescence. How the dirt glinted
and shimmered, how the blind earth
once writhed, alive in your hands.

Monarch

Butterfly, papillon, mariposa. Even the names
for these winged beings flutter off the tongue

light as the papery, painted slips of silk
that carry them across the continent.

They drift down from the trees, dropping
from the bare, pink arms of eucalyptus

to bob and float above the grass, above yucca plants
lifting their spined leaves to the sky.

Above bull thistle, buttercup, sweet fennel, fireweed,
milkweed, the bright flowers of brittlebush.

How can anything so slight exist in the world?
A world that made the tiger, the shark—made us.

I like to watch up close as one uncurls
its spiral straw, sucks nectar from a blossom.

To see the fine black figure, specked with spots.
A polka-dotted dream, grown out of its several bodies.

Fatted, striped. Larval, again and again. Trading
one form for the next as if it were that easy

to be multiple. To slide out of one story, into another.
Oh, to live like that—let go the past with its burdens,

its old hungers, drink the sweetness of the field, then rise,
filigreed, into what must seem endless, possible air.

5

Often, We Love Best

Often, we love best what is hidden: the locket,
our initials etched entwined on the back,
the wool coat's pink silk lining, the painting
beneath a painting, its faint hills and far-off church.
Last month I bought a pitcher, only to discover that,
when tipped to pour, it reveals a hidden message underneath.
We love whatever is inscribed, whatever's whispered
in the delicate shell of the ear. If not the forest, the idea of it—
dense, impenetrable, like the face of someone whose thoughts
we might try and fail to discern, and whom, therefore, we desire.
The lover whose kiss simmers on the back of the neck,
but whose name we hold close to our breast.
The privacy of the womb, its occupant a stirring
beneath the palm. The Holy Grail because of its refusal
to be found. Galaxies not yet seen, but guessed at,
glimmering on the periphery of the universe.
So why not the impossible to know: the shadowed
days ahead, events only sketched on time's parchment,
the fractured gift of age, its slow or quick diminishment,
the last breath. And then after that.

What Begins

What begins in beauty ends in beauty.
What begins in sorrow ends in sorrow.
The seed once planted, soon in full bloom.
If grief, then grief. If anger, anger. They say
the first week of any love affair reveals its end.
Give me the child at seven, and so forth.
The world itself began with a bang. Hard to argue
for another truth. But I have seen a heart
worn thin take to small repairs, have watched
a blue jay born wild eat out of a woman's hand.
And even we began as tadpoles, curled and gilled.
I want to think the starting place is only
one location on a curve that we can follow
to another end. And then, begin again.

The Heart Is Not

a pocket. A thing that
can be turned inside out
by anybody's hand. Not
a place for pebbles or loose
change. Not to carry old
receipts. It does not tear
at the seam. It doesn't have
a seam. It cannot be torn.

Corpse Pose

Lying on the floor, I think of a woman I know
whose ailing father came to her house to die,
but kept on living. He'd putter around,
fix the refrigerator, tinker with the water heater,
patch the peeling plaster in the kitchen.

And though he suffered—was in pain—there always
seemed to be something else to do. *Dad,* she said,
after months of hearing him complain,
why don't you try lying down? Which did the trick.
He took to bed and soon he was gone.

I'd always imagined the end a symphony—
a crescendo, the conductor's arms raised
in that elegant, final pause. But now I see
how little gets resolved. The ceiling leaks,
the novel sits in a drawer, unfinished. And desire,

that constant companion, keeps tossing us
another bone. Like when a woman
told my friend, who was on his deathbed,
that she'd always had a crush on him.
Me too, he said (and after a pause),
Funny we should mention it now.

Painting

for Eduardo Carrillo

Eggs clustered in an African basket. The purple spikes
of onion flowers sticking out of pale blue bottles,
lined up at the windowsill. My own face
reflected in the splotched mirror as I traced my profile
with the tip of a boar-hair brush.

Sometimes, a man or woman would walk in and,
as if on cue, take off all their clothes to lie down
on a podium and lounge for hours.

Now and then, he'd walk over, Ed,
stroke his beard, squint over the arc of his thumb
and mutter something about the light,

then drift into talk of Madrid. *We had to mix
our own pigments from powder,* he said, *make brushes
out of hair cut from the hind legs of a wild dog.*

We never knew whether he was telling the truth straight
or slant. But we didn't care.

Kurt Cobain echoed off the steel rafters,
flies buzzed in and out the open doors. Cows
grazed in the field nearby, lowing softly to their young.

And always the sharp smell of turpentine, the oils:
alizarin crimson, cadmium yellow, titanium white.
Colors we squeezed from their aluminum tubes
onto our palettes.

Up the hill, scientists bent over petri dishes,
examining the outlines of injured cells. Singers
practiced scales, climbing up and down the steep
ladders of their vocal cords.

Somewhere across the globe, our country's bombs
fell on villages, the choke of dust and smoke.

What privilege, unearned—at least by us—
to toil, for that brief season,
beneath our teacher's watchful gaze,
studying the exact way the light
shuddered through the dirty windowpane
onto the tender bodies of Things,
casting its bruised shadows over the given world.

Starsight

Yesterday we went to a flower farm tucked away right
in the middle of a regular neighborhood—acres of snapdragons,
sweet peas, cosmos, an elderberry tree with its small, green clusters
of unripe fruit. We wandered around for hours—me and my friends—
smelling everything and taking pictures of each other taking pictures
of the rows of pink and white, the fluttering clusters of blue. Sometimes
a gopher came up and pulled down a patch of dry grass, and sometimes
the ghost of my brother appeared between the rows, looking sad,
looking like he would have liked to have been there. I've lived a lot
since he died and he knows it. I'm sure he's lived a lot too, but in clouds.
The garden was so beautiful. Hawks flew overhead and a swallowtail butterfly
with wings like a tiger landed in the buddleia. "Can we just stay here?"
I asked out loud. And then I said, "It hurts to love the world," and my brother
nodded, and the two of us just stared at the grove of eucalyptus, light
coming through the crescent leaves and pods, the flowers just now
aching into bloom. If you look, really look at a tree, you can barely stand it.

Today the Pleasures

Today the pleasures are too numerous to name.
Walking over the bridge and up the drive
to get the mail, then setting down the packages
to open by the front door, a fat swath of sun
falling against my arm as I open a box
of two slim books, then a box
with blue ink refills for my favorite pen,
one that glides so nicely across the pages
of my grief. *All this,* I think, *all this,* and also
the broccoli soup I made with bone broth
from last month's turkey, blended to a creamy green.
Yes, the world is falling down, death taking
a stroll down every street. And yes, it's getting hotter
by the hour. And still, today the wind
has quieted and the dogs next door announce
their gods, who, so far, keep lifting the sun
and letting down (just enough) rain.

The Boxes

It's a faint memory now—a hot day in June,
a stranger's house on a hill. Packing the sheets,
the towels, the books. Myself and others—no evidence

of blood or spilled pills on the rug. No length of rope
hanging from the rafters. Only the stale dishes, left in the sink,
and by the door, boots, still crusted with dirt.

I tried not to look at her, the sister, bereft, her face
flushed and blank as she moved about the room,
picking things up, putting them back down, tossing them
into the boxes on the floor.

I kept my eyes downcast, an interloper, trespassing
among the ruins. And all the while, I felt—how
to name it?—the small, immodest flower
of helpfulness bloom in my chest.

How could I have known then that I, too, would pack away
my brother's life in cardboard squares,
gather the impossible burden of his shirts, his shoes,
the black leather jacket that still smelled of his cologne.

I can almost recall one or two (the babysitter? her friend?)
hovering around—as I once did—safe in the periphery.
Going about the motions without having to enter the story.
And worse, feeling better, having done their part

to erase him. Though, in truth, what would
I have done without them, passing from room
to room, busying themselves with purpose,
the fragrance of their innocence buffering the air.

Pool

Last Friday I went to a friend's house because her grandson
was turning one and our surfer friend Vinty was there
and the friend's daughter and all the husbands and it must have been
over ninety degrees, so hot we had to nearly force ourselves to make
our way up the dirt road to their pool and I didn't have a swimsuit
so I stripped down to my skivvies which were super see-through
and I didn't really even care. There were lemon trees growing
alongside the pool like a hedge—so many lemons! And someone
picked some for the baby and he kept dunking them under water
and watching them bob back up with a "pop!" which made him so happy
he would squeal. It was like that: lemons, baby, hot sun, and barn swallows
diving toward the water, skimming the surface to wet their claws
so they could go build mud houses in the eaves. I kept thinking
about the time when I was three and almost drowned at a friend's house,
but the light coming through the water was so beautiful I wasn't afraid,
my parents talking, clinking glasses while I sat on the bottom tiles
and watched the diamonds shimmer, but then my friend's mom,
who is Hawaiian, dove in and scooped me out with her strong arms,
so I lived to be here decades later, watching a naked baby
splash the surface with his palms, in the seventh month
of the year, in the late Anthropocene, everyone laughing
and getting a little burned even beneath the brims of their
sun hats, lemons—lemons everywhere we look.

(R)egret

I see the word *egret,* but read, instead,
        regret. A trick of the mind. Its reversals. One
a white slash, rising from the marsh. The other

a stone, strapped to the heart. The way I've carried
        all the would-haves, all the ifs. Each alternate
exhausts. The egret wades in the dark water,

seeking fish. The heart, constancy. I doubt the egret
        has regrets. Hatch, fledge, breed, hunt.
And besides, a lovely name that comes from French.

Aigrette for "brush," after the long feathers
        that stream down its back. How do its legs,
bent reversed, move ahead? Who wouldn't want

to walk like that? There are days I step
        outside my body, arise, fly over the field
of my life, and glimpse—not error—but river,

rock, and oak. A wide expanse. Here and there
        a meadow, dry grass dotted with—could
they be poppies?—some bright-blurred orange flame.

Haunts

These days we like to walk the old neighborhood,
down the crisscross streets by the dog park, past
the harbor, past Linda's Seabreeze Cafe, past my old house,
a not-much-to-look-at beach shack built for summer,
where the ghost of me still tends my old life: roses
in the garden, laundry on the line, my son in his wheelchair,
head tilted up as I spoon that morning's purée.
I can still hear the neighbor warming up his diesel truck,
the clack of kids next door setting their skateboards
on the sidewalk. At night, the saltwater lament
of seals as I lie in bed looking out the window
at the shadowed green. It's been a year. Or ten. No—
twenty. A man I did not know then holds my hand
as we pass the front yard where the new people
have planted coppertip, daylilies, Mexican sage.
I miss the way the light came through the living room
at midday. The pine out front they had to cut down
because it wanted to lift the house up by the foundation,
into the air. I thought there was another life, a better one.
My son's eyes were dark as earth. We had to hold him close
at night in case he had a seizure. I would have said, then,
it was torture to love someone you couldn't save. But
what did I know? How lucky it was—how lucky
it always is—to love someone at all.

Night Bird

Hear me: Sometimes thunder is just thunder.
The dog barking is only a dog. Leaves fall
from the trees because the days are getting shorter,
by which I mean, not the days we have left,
but the actual length of time, given the tilt of Earth
and distance from the sun. My nephew used to see
a therapist who mentioned that, at play,
he sunk a toy ship and tried to save the captain.
Not, he said, that we want to read anything into that.
Who can read the world? Its paragraphs
of cloud, and alphabets of dust. Just now
a night bird outside my window made a single
plaintive cry that wafted up between the trees.
Not, I'm sure, that it was meant for me.

Let Rain Be Rain

Let rain be rain.
      Let wind be wind.
Let the small stone
      be the small stone.

May the bird
      rest on its branch,
the beetle in its burrow.

May the pine tree
      lay down its needles.
The rockrose, its petals.

It's early. Or it's late.
      The answers
to our questions
      lie hidden
in acorn, oyster, the seagull's
      speckled egg.

We've come this far, already.
      Why not let breath
be breath. Salt be salt.

How faithful the tide
      that has carried us—
that carries us now—
         out to sea
      and back.

Acknowledgments

Gratitude to the following journals where these poems first appeared, sometimes in earlier forms:

Academy of American Poets Poem-a-Day: "Nothing Wants to Suffer"

The Adirondack Review: "Clydesdales," "Corpse Pose," "Horse Heart"

Alaska Quarterly Review: "Blue Note," "What Begins"

The American Poetry Review: "Alphabet of the Apocalypse," "Barefoot," "Hair of the Dead," "Haunts," "Nocturne," "Prayer to Be Undone," "To Break"

Catamaran: "Painting," "Pool"

The Comstock Review: "Starsight"

Gettysburg Review: "The Cows of Love Creek," "Glass," "Monarch"

Grist: "*Haute Potato*"

Jung Journal: "There"

The Kenyon Review: "Okra"

New Ohio Review: "(R)egret"

Pedestal Magazine: "Today the Pleasures"

Ploughshares: "Daughter," "Often, We Love Best," "Slither"

Plume Poetry 10: "They Say the Heart Wants"

Poetry: "Night Bird"

Prairie Schooner: "Praying Mantis"

Rattle: "Appointment"

Reed Magazine: "The Boxes"

RHINO: "Everything Is Old," "How Often One Death"

River Styx: "Boy," "Wind"

The Southern Review: "The Bermuda Triangle," "Construction," "For the Record," "Leg"

The Sun: "The Bugs of Childhood," "Lava"

Gratitude to Montage Health for commissioning the poem "Let Rain Be Rain," which is shared in the waiting room of the Carol Hatton Breast Care Center; to *Plume* for resharing "The Boxes" online; to Jane Hirshfield for selecting "Nothing Wants to Suffer" for Poem-a-Day, as well as "They Say the Heart Wants" for *Plume Poetry 10;* to the New York Public Library for prompting "The Heart Is Not" as a "pocket poem" and James Crews for publishing it in *The Path to Kindness: Poems of Connection and Joy* (Storey Publishing, 2022); to editors Bill Henderson, Ruth Wittman, Jane Hirshfield, and Susan Terris, as well as all other contributing editors, for the inclusion of "Night Bird" in *The Pushcart Prize XLIX: Best of the Small Presses 2025 Edition;* to the Money for Women/Barbara Deming Memorial Fund for their financial contribution; to Terrapin Books for publishing "The Kissing Disease" in *A Constellation of Kisses* (2019); and specially to editors Lee Sioles, Marie Landau, Alison Lockhart, and Jessica Roeder for putting close eyes on the manuscript, along with Copper Canyon editors Ashley E. Wynter and Claretta Holsey. To Ryo Yamaguchi for his enthusiasm, camaraderie, and expertise in guiding the book toward publication. To Armando for being my first reader. And to Joseph Millar and Dorianne Laux, in whose epic backyard some of these poems were written or inspired.

All books are born in community, both with the living and the dead. I am thankful for the poets who have opened the way to what is possible on the page. And, as always, I am indebted to the many editors who have supported the work, journal by journal, poem by poem.

A deep bow to Michael Wiegers for taking this manuscript under the Copper Canyon wing and sharing it with the larger world.

And, most of all, in appreciation of the readers who walk this path with me, one line at a time.

About the Author

Danusha Laméris is an American poet, born to a Dutch father and Barbadian mother and raised in Northern California. Her first book, *The Moons of August* (Autumn House, 2014), was chosen by Naomi Shihab Nye as the winner of the Autumn House Press Poetry Prize and was a finalist for the Milt Kessler Poetry Book Award. A Pushcart Prize winner, she is also the author of *Bonfire Opera* (University of Pittsburgh Press, Pitt Poetry Series, 2020), a finalist for the 2021 Paterson Poetry Prize and recipient of the 2021 Northern California Book Award in Poetry. Some of her work has been published in *The Best American Poetry, The New York Times, The American Poetry Review, The Sun, Poetry, Prairie Schooner, Ploughshares, Orion, The Kenyon Review,* and *The American Scholar.* As the Santa Cruz County, California, Poet Laureate, she cofounded The Hive Poetry Collective, a radio show, podcast, and event hub. Laméris is on the faculty of Pacific University's Low-Residency MFA Program. www.danushalameris.com.

Poetry is vital to language and living. Since 1972, Copper Canyon Press has published extraordinary poetry from around the world to engage the imaginations and intellects of readers, writers, booksellers, librarians, teachers, students, and donors.

WE ARE GRATEFUL FOR THE MAJOR SUPPORT PROVIDED BY:

academy of american poets

OFFICE OF ARTS & CULTURE
SEATTLE

ARTSFUND

THE PAUL G. ALLEN
FAMILY FOUNDATION

Hawthornden Foundation

POETRY FOUNDATION

INGRAM CONTENT GROUP

the point
envision · enact · evolve

McSWEENEY'S

WASHINGTON STATE
ARTS COMMISSION

National Endowment for the Arts
arts.gov

The Witter Bynner Foundation
for Poetry

TO LEARN MORE ABOUT UNDERWRITING
COPPER CANYON PRESS TITLES,
PLEASE CALL 360-385-4925 EXT. 105

WE ARE GRATEFUL FOR THE MAJOR SUPPORT PROVIDED BY:

Anonymous

Jill Baker and Jeffrey Bishop

Anne and Geoffrey Barker

Donna Bellew

Will Blythe

John Branch

Diana Broze

Sarah J. Cavanaugh

Keith Cowan and Linda Walsh

Peter Currie

The Evans Family

Mimi Gardner Gates

Gull Industries Inc.
    on behalf of William True

Carolyn and Robert Hedin

David and Jane Hibbard

Bruce S. Kahn

Phil Kovacevich and Eric Wechsler

Maureen Lee and Mark Busto

Ellie Mathews and Carl Youngmann
    as The North Press

Larry Mawby and Lois Bahle

Petunia Charitable Fund and
    adviser Elizabeth Hebert

Suzanne Rapp and Mark Hamilton

Adam and Lynn Rauch

Emily and Dan Raymond

Joseph C. Roberts

Cynthia Sears

Kim and Jeff Seely

Tree Swenson

Julia Sze

Barbara and Charles Wright

In honor of C.D. Wright
    from Forrest Gander

Caleb Young as C. Young Creative

The dedicated interns and faithful
    volunteers of Copper Canyon Press

The pressmark for Copper Canyon Press
suggests entrance, connection, and interaction
while holding at its center
an attentive, dynamic space for poetry.

This book is set in Plantin.
Book design by Phil Kovacevich.
Printed on archival-quality paper.